SMARTGUIDE

decorative
paint techniques
step-by-step projects

CREATIVE HOMEOWNER®, Upper Saddle River, New Jersey

Creative Homeowner® and **SMART**GUIDE® are registered trademarks of Federal Marketing Corporation.

VP / Editorial Director: Timothy O. Bakke
Production Managers: Kimberly H. Vivas, Rose Sullivan

Senior Editor: Kathie Robitz
Editorial Assistants: Lauren Manoy, Evan Lambert

Senior Designer: David Geer
Photography: George Ross / CH
Stencil Illustrations: Tina Basile
Cover Design: Clarke Barre

Manufactured in the United States of America

Current Printing (last digit)
10 9 8 7 6 5 4 3 2 1

Smart Guide: Decorative Paint Techniques
Library of Congress Control Number: 2004103752
ISBN: 1-58011-213-7

CREATIVE HOMEOWNER®
A Division of Federal Marketing Corp.
24 Park Way
Upper Saddle River, NJ 07458
www.creativehomeowner.com

Metric Conversion

Length

1 inch	25.4 mm
1 foot	0.3048 m
1 yard	0.9144 m
1 mile	1.61 km

Area

1 square inch	645 mm^2
1 square foot	0.0929 m^2
1 square yard	0.8361 m^2
1 acre	4046.86 m^2
1 square mile	2.59 km^2

Volume

1 cubic inch	16.3870 cm^3
1 cubic foot	0.03 m^3
1 cubic yard	0.77 m^3

Common Lumber Equivalents

Sizes: Metric cross sections are so close to their U.S. sizes, as noted below, that for most purposes they may be considered equivalents.

Dimensional	1 × 2	19 × 38 mm
lumber	1 × 4	19 × 89 mm
	2 × 2	38 × 38 mm
	2 × 4	38 × 89 mm
	2 × 6	38 × 140 mm
	2 × 8	38 × 184 mm
	2 × 10	38 × 235 mm
	2 × 12	38 × 286 mm

Capacity

1 fluid ounce	29.57 mL
1 pint	473.18 mL
1 quart	1.14 L
1 gallon	3.79 L

Weight

1 ounce	28.35g
1 pound	0.45kg

Temperature

Fahrenheit = Celsius × 1.8 + 32
Celsius = Fahrenheit – 32 × ⅝

Nail Size & Length

Penny Size	Nail Length
2d	1"
3d	1¼"
4d	1½"
5d	1¾"
6d	2"
7d	2¼"
8d	2½"
9d	2¾"
10d	3"
12d	3¼"
16d	3½"

contents

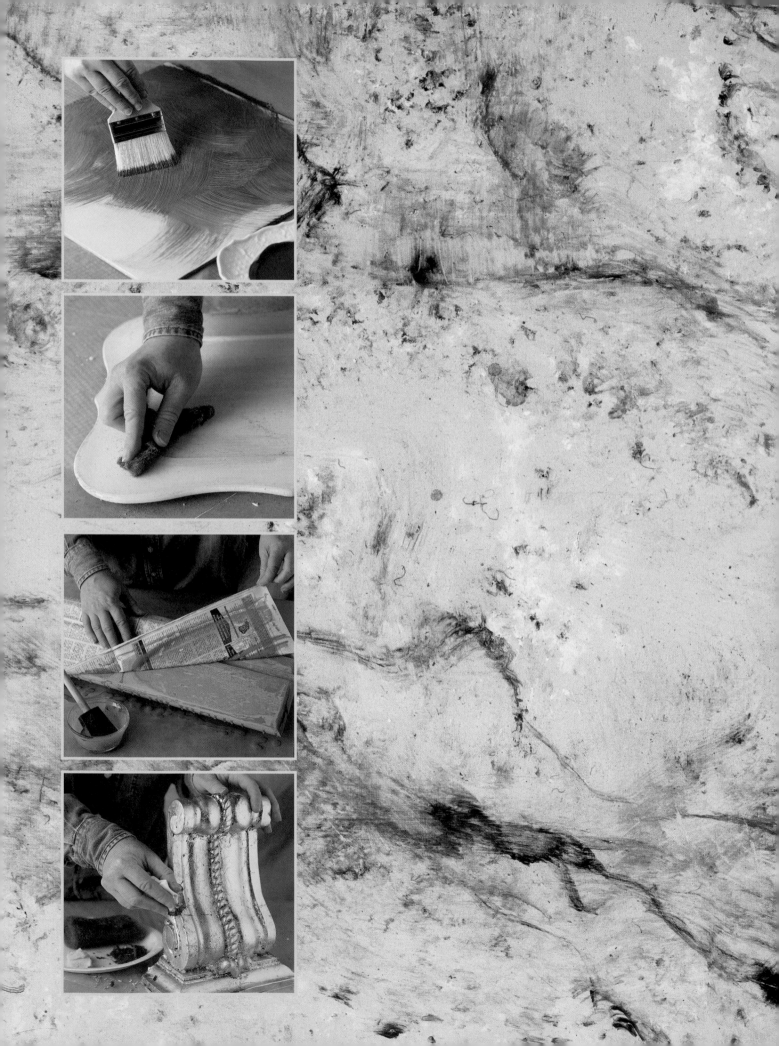

the basics

chapter 1
preparation and equipment

The Workshop

Not having a well-equipped workshop shouldn't discourage you from doing any of the projects in this book. While it's important to have a clean, well-ventilated space with good lighting, you can set up a temporary work area in an unused corner in the basement or an extra room, in part of the garage, or even in the backyard. Wherever it is, you'll need a work surface. If you decide to transform your kitchen or dining room, protect the table with several layers of brown kraft paper. Some hardware stores carry it in big sheets that can be used as drop cloths. If you can't find sheets, the paper is widely available rolled on a tube. After covering the table with paper, spread a clear plastic tarp over that, and secure it with masking tape. When the plastic gets messy, as it surely will, replace it with another sheet.

Planning ahead is the key to completing a project quickly. Take inventory of what you'll need before you even begin. There is nothing more frustrating than having to stop your work to run out to the hardware store for steel wool because you assumed that you already had some. At the end of this chapter is a shopping list of general materials.

Paint Mixing and Storage

Paint is basic to these techniques. Glass dessert dishes, small mixing bowls, or plastic storage containers are all ideal for mixing paint. Save the plastic lidded containers from salad bars. They provide a clever solution to the problem of paint drying up when you can't finish something in one session. When you've completed a project, return any unused paint to its original package or store it in a tightly sealed container. When working with small amounts of multiple colors, use a palette. If you don't have an artist's watercolor palette, coated paper plates make good disposable substitutes. When mixing a new shade of paint, always save a small amount to use for touching up any imperfections that may occur before you apply the sealer coat. Bamboo chopsticks and tongue depressors make good mixing sticks for stirring small amounts of paint. The paint sticks given out at hardware stores are fine for stirring large quantities.

Brushes and Other Tools

Without a doubt, the most important tools for applying painted finishes are, of course, brushes. **Paintbrushes** vary widely in both quality and price. Traditional professional paint finishes often involve labor-intensive, multiple-step techniques and employ difficult-to-use oil- or shellac-based ingredients. In addition, the special tools and brushes needed for many of these methods are an investment in themselves. This book tries to keep materials and steps simple so that you don't have to spend $100 for a badger brush when a $10 soft bristle brush will suffice. It's a good idea to purchase several good **artist's brushes, stencil brushes** in a couple of sizes, a **dragging brush,** and **stippler, spatter, liner, pointed, and round brushes.**

Disposable **foam brushes** are a fabulous innovation with numerous advantages, including their low cost. Foam brushes don't leave brush marks on your work, and there's no risk of bristles falling out and getting stuck in the wet paint. They do have limitations, though, so don't attempt to use them for absolutely everything. For example, on surfaces with many crevices, **bristle brushes** will provide the best overall coverage. Also, foam brushes wear out quickly and must be replaced often, which probably explains why they are available by the bagful!

Artist's Brushes

Assorted Paintbrushes

Fine Brushes

Foam Brushes

Dragging Brush

Always keep a supply of old towels and soft cotton rags around. They come in handy for both cleaning up and applying some techniques. Also keep paper towels, **sponges,** and clean water close at hand. If there isn't a sink in your work area, keep a bucket of water on the floor nearby.

A **pencil** or, better yet, a chalk pencil is good for marking the placement of motifs or images. Chalk lines can be wiped off easily, which lets you make changes without ruining the base coat or the background finish.

Additional Supplies

Many projects and techniques require working one section at a time. Cover the adjacent sections with low-tack **masking tape** to protect them from paints. For a large area, tape a sheet of paper over the surface.

You can also use masking tape or a ruler to mark guidelines that are necessary to keep motifs straight or level. Use a **craft knife** if you have to cut the masking tape around shapes or corners. Burnish the tape's edges diligently to prevent paints from seeping underneath. Afterward, carefully remove the masking tape before the paint is thoroughly dry. You can touch up any fuzzy edges with a fine paintbrush.

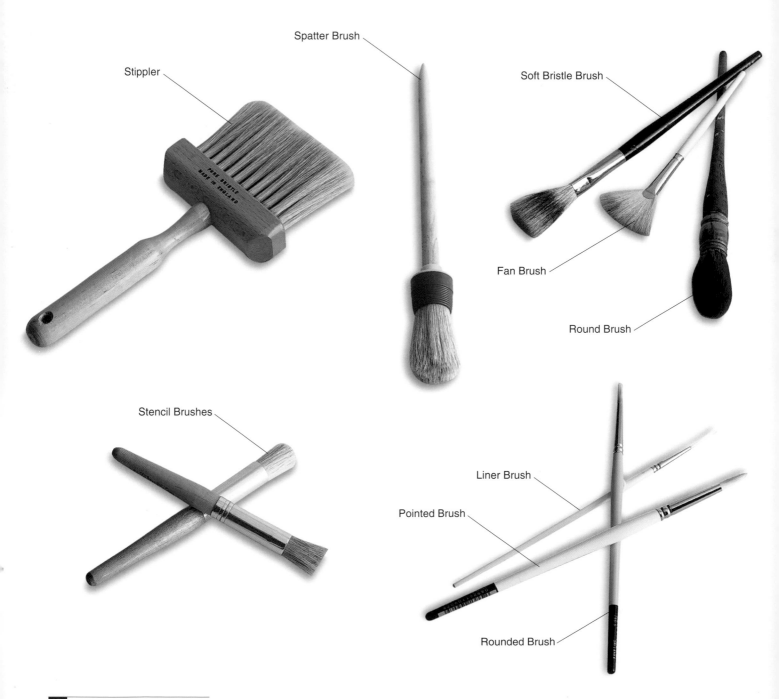

Stippler

Spatter Brush

Soft Bristle Brush

Fan Brush

Round Brush

Stencil Brushes

Liner Brush

Pointed Brush

Rounded Brush

Preparing Wood Surfaces.
Wooden objects will generally require sanding or smoothing before finishes are applied. If there is an existing finish on the surface, remove any loose or flaking portions. Avoid working on furniture that has a finish that needs to be stripped unless you don't mind applying elbow grease to this extra step. In that case, carefully follow the manufacturer's instructions for the stripping agent you select, and wear sturdy **gloves** and a **mask.** Also, make sure the place where you are working is well-ventilated.

Wash very dirty items with trisodium phosphate (TSP), which is available at hardware stores, and a **scrub brush.** Allow everything to dry completely before sanding or painting. Fill in holes and cracks with wood putty, as necessary. Sand down the surface with three grades of **sandpaper.** You may want to use an electric sander on large flat surfaces. Begin with a coarse grade of 60- or 100-grit sandpaper, and finish with a finer grade of 150- or 200-grit sandpaper. Always wipe the surface clean with tack cloths after sanding.

The Media

Most of the projects and techniques featured in this book are done with latex **primers, paints,** and **glazes,** which are easier to work with, faster-drying, and environmentally safer than their oil-based counterparts. These products have the added advantage of easy cleaning. You can quickly clean brushes loaded with latex paint with warm water. For brushes that have been used with oil-based paints, you'll have to clean them with paint thinner, then wash them out with mild soap and warm water.

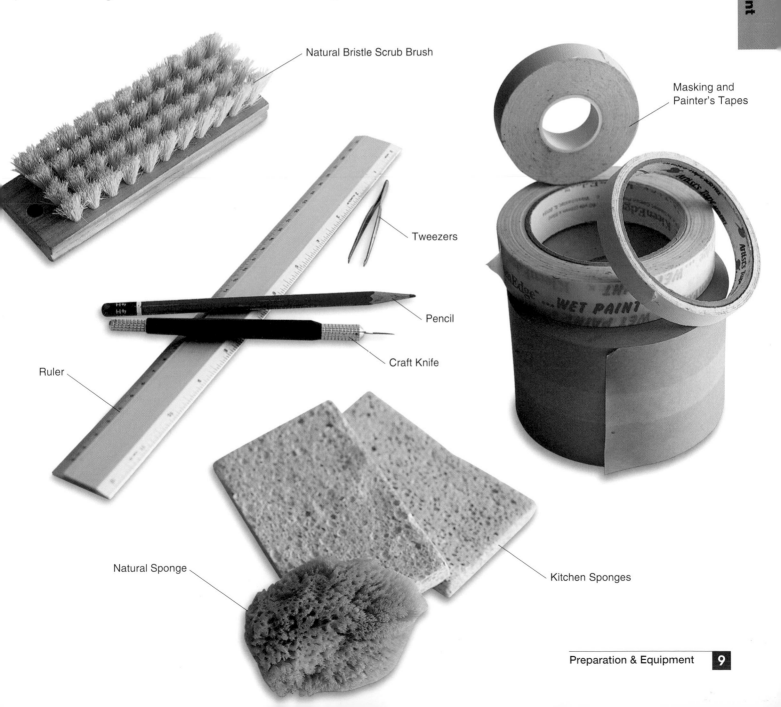

Natural Bristle Scrub Brush

Masking and Painter's Tapes

Tweezers

Pencil

Craft Knife

Ruler

Natural Sponge

Kitchen Sponges

Priming. Most surfaces will need at least one coat of primer before painting with the base color. Use a good-quality, multipurpose latex primer. This will ensure that the paint will adhere not soak into the surface and create a blotchy appearance. Next, cover the surface with one or two coats of the base color. For certain projects, a heavy-duty, shellac-based primer is recommended to camouflage really stubborn stains and knots. In some cases, the wood grain is meant to show through. These items don't require priming. Always use a metal primer on metal objects, following the manufacturer's instructions for preparing the surface and application. If the piece is rusty, go over it with a scraper, wire brush, or steel wool prior to priming. When working with spray paints, it's especially important to keep the worplace well-ventilated. Some people prefer to use spray paint outdoors only, but wind can make doing so difficult.

Glazing. A glaze adds depth and richness to a base color. By definition, a glaze will always be translucent, no matter how dark the shade is. Traditionally, glazes were always oil-based and usually involved a time-consuming multiple application process to achieve depth and richness. In recent years, water-based glazes have been developed that fairly successfully mimic the look obtained by oil glazing. While they don't give the same rich patina that a true oil-based glaze would, premixed acrylic glazes are used here for some projects. If you prefer to create your own, mix acrylic paints with a neutral glaze and a thinner until you get the shade you desire.

Sandpaper

Steel Wool

Primers, Paints, and Glazes

Protective Gloves and Dust Mask

Important Tips

When trying a new technique—especially with **combs, stencils, stamps,** or **sponges**—practice on a sanded board before actually beginning the project. A 16-inch square of plywood is an ideal surface that is still a manageable size but large enough to really show the finished effect of the technique.

If you don't have access to a table saw, most lumberyards will cut a sheet of plywood into squares for you.

Some techniques require manipulation while the paint or glaze is still wet. Do these one section at a time. Keep the outside edge wet so that you can smoothly feather it into the next section without creating a hard break or line in the finish.

Allow the paints to dry before proceeding to the next step, unless otherwise noted. When stenciling, do not reposition your stencil or work on another section before the paint is dry to the touch in order to prevent smudges or smears.

Rubber Stamps

Foam Shape

Plastic Combs

Stencils

Shopping List

In addition to specific brushes and materials required for each technique, stock these supplies:

- Kraft paper
- Clear plastic drop cloth
- Wood putty or wood filler
- Sandpaper: 3 different grades
- Steel wool
- Tack cloths
- Multipurpose primer
- Heavy-duty primer
- Mineral spirits
- Sponges: natural and cellulose
- Masking or painter's tape
- Craft knife
- Plastic or glass mixing containers in assorted sizes
- Mixing sticks

Certain projects in this book include highlighting or adding an antique effect. They will require working with **liquid gold, liquid gilding, gold wax,** or **metal leaf.** In most cases, your aim will be to apply a bit of faded glory rather than all-out glitz, so don't worry about creating a smooth, even coat. If it looks worn, it's all the better.

On wooden pieces you can go over the finish with a **cheesecloth** and **furniture wax.** Other projects may call for "aging" wood with **antiquing wax, shoe polish,** or **candle wax.**

Protecting The Finish
When your paint project is completed, seal it with two or more coats of a water-based clear top coat. (Always allow paints to dry for 24 hours in order to cure completely before applying a sealer to the finish.) A clear top coat is just that— a transparent finishing layer of protection. Some decorative painting techniques—sponging, color washing, and stenciling, to name a few—don't necessarily

need a clear top coat because they provide a durable surface by themselves. As a general rule, you might apply a clear top coat as protection over any decorative painted surface in hard-use living areas, such as a kitchen, in a child's bedroom, or on floors, woodwork, doors, countertops, or tables, which are prone to wear and tear.

Complex finishes, such as marbling, always require a clear top coat. It gives the faux stone a depth that adds to its realism as well as providing protection.

Polyurethane. This product makes a good top coat for most kinds of paint. However, polyurethane will yellow, and so it is particularly troublesome when used over white, pastels, and subtle color combinations. Fortunately, polyurethane does not affect black and dark colors to the same degree.

Acrylic Varnish. You can use acrylic varnish over any water-soluble paints, such as acrylics or

latex products. This top coat will dry quickly, but it yellows slightly. As with polyurethane, yellowing is not visible over black- or other dark-painted surfaces.

Water-Based Polyurethane. If you want to preserve the color of a painted finish, you must use a water-based polyurethane. It's strong and takes a bit longer to dry than acrylic varnish, but it produces no yellowing.

Condition Your Brushes

Don't let stray bristles mar your finish. When you buy a new brush, remove loose hairs. Wash the brush in warm soapy water. While it is still damp, move the bristles back and forth in your hand, and spin the brush between your palms so that any more loose bristles will work their way into sight, for you to pick them out.

- Paint palettes or coated paper plates

- Paper towels

- Newspaper

- Soft lint-free cloths
(such as old cotton T-shirts)

- Pencils

- Ruler or straightedge

- Measuring tape

- Acrylic sealer in satin or gloss finish

Three shades of green-tinted glaze have been applied to this trio of wooden band boxes. The finish was sealed with a top coat of non-yellowing water-based polyurethane.

Cheesecloth

Furniture Wax

Liquid Gilding

Candle Wax

Antiquing Wax

Liquid Gold

Shoe Polish

Metal Leaf

Gold Wax

chapter 2

color selection

The Importance of Color

The most creative tool you can use with any decorative paint technique is color. Whether you're working on a large surface or a small object, your choice of color can have the greatest impact on the overall result. What you select may depend on the technique, how well the color harmonizes with other colors nearby, and how successfully it complements the object you are painting, or in the case of a wall or large architectural feature, whether the color complements the room's style. On the other hand, your choice may be less studied, because color is a personal preference above all else. And yet, without delving too deeply into the science of color, learning a bit about color theory can be beneficial, especially if your project is a large one.

Understanding and Using Color

Color is your perception of light as it is reflected by an object. Reflected light travels from the object, such as a flower, to your optic nerve in wavelengths. The color you "see" depends on the number and length of the light waves. For example, paint contains a substance called pigment, which reflects light waves of varying lengths that create different colors.

Color can be described by three qualities: *hue* (another name for a specific color or a color family); *value* (a color's lightness or darkness), and *intensity* (how bright or dull a color appears). There are several ways to lessen a color's intensity. You can lighten it with white to form a *tint* (below left), darken it with black to create a *shade* (below right), or add gray to arrive at a *tone*. Tinting gives color a lighter value, and shading, of course, makes it darker.

Color Intensity

Tint	Shade

Color Wheel Combinations

Basic Color Wheel

Analogous

Complements

Split Complements

Triad

Tetrad

combine a primary with a secondary to create green-blue, orange-yellow, and so on.

Refer to the color wheel (top left) to help you envision certain color combinations you may want to use for your project. An *analogous* color scheme (top right) involves neighboring colors that share an underlying hue. *Complementary* colors (middle left) are opposite each other on the color wheel and often work well together. If they look too strong in their full value, use the lighter shades or varying intensities of the same two colors. A *double complementary* scheme involves an additional set of opposites, such as green-blue and red-orange.

Alternatively, you could choose a monochromatic scheme or palette, which involves using one color in a variety of intensities. Another way to create a monochromatic scheme is to use different finishes of the same paint color—painting stripes by alternating a high-gloss finish with a matte finish of the same hue, for instance.

A *split complement* (middle right) is composed of three colors—one primary or intermediate and two colors on either side of its opposite. For example, instead of teaming purple with yellow, shift the mix to purple with orange-yellow and yellow-green. If you want a more complex palette of three or more colors, look at the *triads* (bottom left), which are formed by three equidistant colors, such as red/yellow/blue or green/purple/orange.

Lastly, if you're daring, try a palette of four colors, equally spaced around the wheel, called a *tetrad* (bottom right). Remember, colors do not have to be used full strength—yellow can be cream, red can be a pale pink, and orange can be a soft peach.

You may have heard designers and color experts refer to something called the *color wheel*, which is simply a representation of pigment colors as a circle. It's a useful reference when you are selecting colors to pair with one another in a color scheme. There are 12 pure colors depicted on the color wheel. They are divided into three groups: the *primaries* red, blue, and yellow; the *secondaries*, which combine two primaries to make green, orange, or violet; and the *intermediates*, which

Finally, there are the *neutral* colors. These include the three classics: white, black, and gray. Technically, white and black are noncolors, and pure gray results from mixing white and black. Another category of neutrals are the "earth tones." These consist of the browns and other neutral colors found in nature.

How to Choose Paint Colors

If you've ever wondered how many paint colors there are, take a look at any paint manufacturer's color-chip system in a home center or paint store. The number is incredible, but it illustrates how many subtle variations on one hue can be achieved.

Everybody has a favorite color. But for many people, choosing a paint color, or more specifically the right shade of a color, is vexing. It pays off to take your time before you make a color decision, especially if your project is large.

Of course, using colors that spontaneously attract you is a good idea because they make you feel comfortable naturally. But you should also think about what you will be painting and whether the colors you have in mind are suitable for the application. If you will be applying a faux technique, for example, choose colors that come closest to those found in the real thing. Study natural wood or stone. Look for variations in shading and tones.

Color and Perception

If you're selecting an overall palette for a room, think about how color will affect the way the room looks and feels. Each color has a distinct personality that is partly dictated by

its temperature—warm or cool—but also influenced by cultural or emotional factors—"green with envy" or "rosy with optimism."

In general, warm colors (red, yellow, and orange) and dark shades advance, which means they may make a small room feel even smaller. On the other hand, they can also make a room that's large or sparsely furnished feel cozy. Warm hues enliven a space, so they are excellent choices for rooms where there is a lot of activity. Kitchens, playrooms, the home office, and craft or hobby rooms are all good examples, as is any spot in the house that needs to be brightened.

The opposite happens when you use cool colors (blue, green, and violet) and light tones. These colors recede, which means that they can make small or crowded rooms seem more spacious, open, and airy. Cool hues tend to be soothing and restful, which is why they are perfect for bedrooms, home spas, or any other place in the house that needs toning down.

Light and Color. Lighting can change color dramatically. Before you apply color to a wall, test it. Buy a small amount, and paint a sample on the wall. Look at it during the daytime to see how it changes with the natural night. Then check it at night to see how it looks when you've turned on the light fixtures.

With less technical jargon, the color combinations fall into these two basic categories:

■ *harmonious*, or *analogous*, schemes, derived from nearby colors on the wheel—less than halfway around; and

■ *contrasting*, or *complementary*, schemes, involving colors that are directly opposite each other on the wheel.

More Color Groups

To complete your color repertoire, there are two more color groups for consideration. *Complex* colors are made by combining two secondary colors to form a *tertiary* color (purple plus orange creates brown). Blend two tertiary colors and you'll create a *quaternary* color. Complex colors are subtler and richer than pure hues.

red

Red is powerful, dramatic, and motivating. It's also hospitable and stimulates the appetite, which makes it a favorite for dining rooms. Some studies have indicated that a red room actually makes people feel warmer.

2 Color Selection

blue

Blue is associated with the sea and sky. It offers serenity, which is why it is a favorite for bedrooms. Studies have shown that people think better in blue rooms. Cooler blues show this color's melancholy side, however.

yellow

Color and Home Decorating

Yellow illuminates the colors it surrounds. It warms rooms that face north (and, therefore, receive no direct sunlight), but it can be too bright in a sunny room. Yellow is cheerful and works best for daytime rooms, not bedrooms.

green

Green is nature's dominant color. It symbolizes comfort and plenty. Green is also tranquil, nurturing, and rejuvenating. Because it is a mixture of blue and yellow, green can be cool or warm, depending on the ratio of the two primary colors.

pink

Pink is outgoing and active. It's also a color that flatters skin tones, which may be why it is associated with youth. Hot shades are invigorating, while soft, toned-down versions can be relaxed and charming.

2 Color Selection

violet

Violet is royal and independent. It is also associated with spirituality. As a decorating color, it goes in and out of fashion, and it is best when used as an accent in a light shade or tint.

orange

Orange is festive, hot, and vibrant. It can be overpowering at its fullest intensity, but pale toned-down versions can be lovely and soft. Like red, orange stimulates the appetite and socializing, so use it accordingly.

2 Color Selection

neutrals

Black and **white,** the noncolors, are sophisticated and refined. Used together these absolute contrasts are dramatic and stylish. They go with all colors, which makes them excellent accents.

Gray goes with all colors—it is a good neighbor. Various tones of gray range from dark charcoal to pale oyster. Earth tones are muted and understated, comprised of the various browns and neutrals that are found in nature.

Techniques for Manipulating Space with Color

Just as color has the power to produce physical and emotional changes, it also has the ability to visually mold space. It influences perceptions of size and shape, masks flaws, highlights good points, and creates harmony throughout a house.

1. To alter a room's physical size, paint it a light, cool color to make it seem a bit larger and airier; a dark or warm color will make it seem smaller as well as cozier.

2. To warm north- or east-facing rooms, which tend to be cool and receive weak natural light, decorate them with light or bright and warm colors. To temper south-facing rooms, which tend to get hot, or west-facing rooms, which are bright and warm (especially on summer afternoons), decorate with light, cool colors.

3. To raise a room's visual height, carry the wall color to the ceiling. Paint any crown or cove molding the same color as the walls.

4. To make a high ceiling appear lower or make a room feel more intimate, stop the wall's color 9 to 12 inches below the ceiling, and accent that line with a stenciled border, a wallpaper border, or molding. Or paint the ceiling in a subdued accent shade, bringing it onto the wall 9 to 12 inches below the ceiling line. Then accent the line with a border.

6. To camouflage an unsightly feature, such as a radiator, paint it the same color as the walls so that it seems to disappear.

7. To highlight an attractive feature, such as molding, paint it a color that contrasts with the walls.

8. To unify a house with all-white or all-beige walls, use the same shade in all of the rooms.

9. To create harmony throughout a house, choose a signature color, and use it in some way in each room. Make it the dominant color in one room, the secondary color in another, the accent color in a third, an accessory color in a fourth, and so on.

10. To unify a house in which different hues have been used in each room, use neutral colors in transitional spaces such as hallways. This not only visually separates spaces but also prevents color clashes between rooms.

chapter 3

finishes and techniques

Basic Surfaces

All of these procedures are ways to create texture on either small or large areas. They can be used to create backgrounds for other techniques, such as stenciling, or they can stand on their own. While they have been applied to furniture and accessories in this book, any of these treatments can be done on walls, as well. The introduction of texture to a surface, whether it's intended to cover an entire wall or adorn the smallest accessory, adds depth and visual interest that draws in the eye.

Creating a Color Wash

You will need: Acrylic paint for base coat • Acrylic paint for top coat • Glazing medium • Flat foam paintbrushes • 3-inch flat bristle paintbrush • Mixing container • optional: Third color

Using a flat brush, paint the surface with two coats of the base color, and allow it to dry. Mix the glaze. Apply it to the surface with a bristle brush, making random, uneven strokes. Work across the piece in vertical sections. Move the brush down each section making short, overlapping passes in a zigzag pattern. This builds up a textured crosshatch design with the base coat showing through. You can use additional colors with subsequent coats of glaze, but allow each coat to dry before applying the next one, or the colors will blend together.

Some of these finishes involve adding texture to a surface by applying paint or glaze with a brush, sponge, or bunched-up cloth and allowing some of the base coat to remain visible. With other techniques, such as dragging and frottage, you will be taking away some of the top coat, while it is still wet, to expose the base coat; these finishes are called *subtractive* techniques.

Using contrasting colors for the base and top coats produces a stronger look than using related shades. Buy a premixed glaze in any color, or make a glaze yourself using acrylic paint and a colorless glazing medium. Experiment with the amounts until you get the desired translucent shade.

Combing

You will need: Acrylic paint for base coat • Mixed acrylic glaze • Multipurpose rubber paint comb • Flat foam paintbrushes • Paper towels • Stiff cardboard • Scissors or craft knife • Straightedge or ruler

Paint the surface with the base coat, and allow it to dry; then apply one coat of the glaze to cover it **(step 1)**. Work one small section at a time if the surface area is large. This is important because to create the pattern, you have to move the combing tool through the glaze while it is still wet.

To work this technique, hold the comb at an angle of about 80 degrees. Apply just enough pressure so that the comb bends slightly and cuts through the wet glaze as you pull it toward you in the desired pattern **(step 2)**. Practice on a sample board first. Work wavy or straight lines to create different effects. Go over vertically combed lines with a horizontal pass of the tool for a checkered pattern.

Whatever pattern you finally choose, always keep the comb strokes smooth and steady as you go along. Wipe the comb clean after each pass to offload excess paint. The uneven edges of the tines and the intervals between them will create different textures. If you make a mistake, apply another coat and try again while the glaze is still wet.

If you don't want to purchase the combing tool, you can make a comb from cardboard. It's easy. Cut a rectangle of stiff cardboard that is approximately 4 inches wide. Notch it with a zigzag pattern along one of the long sides of the rectangle to create tines. Just remember that homemade cardboard combs get soggy after a short time, so you may need to make several and have them on hand so that there is no interruption in your work.

If you are painting multiple objects or a moderately large surface, it is worth investing in a rubber comb. This is an inexpensive item that you can easily find in a craft store or hobby shop. For a very large area, such as a wall, try using a notched squeegee. Cut tines to a desired size with a craft knife.

1 Apply glaze over the dry base coat. On large surfaces, work one small section at a time.

2 Hold the comb at an 80-deg. angle, and drag it through the wet glaze toward you. Make curved or straight lines, but keep strokes smooth and steady.

Crackle Glazing

You will need: Acrylic paint for base coat • Acrylic paint for top coat • Crackle medium • Antiquing medium • Paintbrushes • Soft lint-free cloth

Go over the surface with two base coats, and allow it to dry. This is the color that will show between the cracks when the job is finished. It should contrast with the color of the top coat. Using a brush, apply one coat of the crackle medium. Work in smooth strokes, covering the entire surface **(step 1)**. Do not coat the same area twice. The thicker the coat of crackle medium, the wider the cracks will be. Vary the thickness over the surface for the random look of natural aging. Brushing on the medium in various directions will form a more complex pattern, as well. When the crackle medium is *almost* dry, apply one coat of the contrasting paint over the surface **(step 2)**. As it dries, it will curl back in spots to reveal the base-coat **(step 3)**. An option is to rub antiquing medium over the cracks using a soft rag.

1 Brush on one coat of crackle medium. For wide cracks, apply a thick coat; for a subtler affect, use a thin layer of the liquid.

2 Before the crackle medium becomes thoroughly dry, apply the contrasting top coat.

3 The final finish. To accentuate the cracks, rub antiquing medium into them using a soft rag. Wipe away any excess, leaving just enough to lightly highlight the cracks.

Distressing

You will need: Candle wax
• Acrylic paint for the top coat
• Antiquing wax or brown shoe polish
• Sandpaper • Steel wool • Tack
cloths • Flat foam paintbrushes
• Soft lint-free cloths

Like crackle finishing, distressing is a technique that gives the effect of physical wear on wood. Another name for the technique is patina finish because it aims to give new or not very old wooden surfaces the venerable appearance of age. Some people also call it "antiquing." Distressing works well on both unfinished and finished wood. Remove any surface imperfections using fine sandpaper or steel wool. Then go over the surface thoroughly with a clean tack cloth to remove any dust or sanding residue. Once that's done, apply the candle wax, which will act as a resister. Rub it onto selected places on the surface you are finishing to prevent these areas from absorbing paint **(step 1)**. In other words, apply the wax to spots that would most naturally become exposed to wear over time, such as near the edges and on and around the corners and knobs of furniture. (To achieve a realistic result, it's helpful to study furniture or wood that has been exposed to hard wear or the weather.) Cover the entire surface with one coat of paint, and allow it to dry **(step 2)**. Then, with the sandpaper or steel wool, go over the waxed areas to lift off some of the paint **(step 3)**.

1 After sanding the surface to a smooth finish, rub candle wax into any areas where you want to simulate natural wear. Typically, this should be near the edges or at the corners.

2 Apply one coat of acrylic paint to cover the entire surface. Let it dry thoroughly.

3 With steel wool or sandpaper, go back over the waxed areas to scratch off the new paint.

Continued on page 30

3 Finishes and Techniques

Continued from page 29

To intensify the illusion of age, rub the entire surface with a coat of antiquing wax. Apply a little extra in the "worn" spots, scuffing it a bit with a piece of steel wool **(step 4)**. If you don't have antiquing medium, brown shoe polish is an excellent substitute.

4 Rub in a small amount of brown shoe polish or antiquing wax into the "worn" spots. Use steel wool to scuff it.

Dragging

You will need: Acrylic paint for the base coat • Acrylic glaze • Dragging brush or stiff-bristled whisk broom • Flat foam paintbrushes

Paint the surface with two coats of the base color, and allow it to dry. Because the dragging technique must be worked on wet glaze, it is a good idea to work in small sections if the overall surface is large. With that in mind, apply one coat of the glaze **(step 1)**. Hold the handle of the dragging brush at a 45-degree angle above the surface, and pull the bristles through the glaze toward you **(step 2)**. (For larger surfaces, you can use a good-quality, stiff-bristled whisk broom.) Drag the brush slowly, making one uninterrupted pass. Continue onto the next section, overlapping with the wet edge of the previous one so as not to create a distinct break. The lines do not have to be straight. The charm of the technique is that it is supposed to look as if it was done by hand. Usually, the lines are vertical, but they can be horizontal, diagonal, or curved, as well. Make them fine or bold. Create combed, plaited, or crosshatched patterns. The dragging brush must remain relatively dry. When it starts to collect paint, wash and dry it before continuing.

1 After the base coat dries thoroughly, apply one coat of glaze over the surface.

2 Hold the handle of the dragging brush at a 45-deg. angle above the surface, and pull the bristles through the wet glaze toward you.

Frottage

You will need: Acrylic paint for base coat • Acrylic paint for top coat • Newspapers or plastic wrap • Flat foam paintbrushes • Mixing container

Apply two or more base coats, and allow the paint to dry. In the meantime, make a wash of one part paint (using the paint intended for the top coat) and two parts water. The mixture should be the consistency of milk. Because acrylic paint dries quickly and the technique requires a wet surface, work in small sections. First, apply the wash **(step 1)**. Take a large sheet of newspaper, and smooth it over the wet paint. Some newspaper ink comes off easily; if that is the case, use newsprint paper or plain brown wrapping paper. Using your fingers or the palms of your hands, push the paper around in the wet paint to create a pattern **(step 2)**. Immediately, pull the paper off the wet paint **(step 3)**. Go on to the next section. With each one, change the direction in which you remove the paper to add more complexity to the painted texture's appearance. If you are working on a small object or where there are curves or corners, you can substitute plastic wrap for the newspaper. It fits more easily into tight spaces and crevices. Wrinkles and creases in the paper or plastic wrap are desirable and actually enhance the textural look of the finished technique. Paper will absorb some of the thinned paint, but plastic wrap won't, so the effect produced by the two materials will be slightly different.

1 Apply the wash to a small section of the surface over a thoroughly dry base coat or two of paint.

2 Smooth a large sheet of newspaper over the wet paint. Push the paint around with the palm of your hand or your fingers.

3 Immediately lift off the newspaper. Don't wait for the paint to become dry.

Ragging

You will need: Acrylic paint for the base coat • Acrylic glaze for the top coat • Flat foam paint-brushes • Soft lint-free cloths

Paint the surface with two coats of the base color, and allow it to dry. This is another technique that requires a wet top coat of glaze, so divide the surface or object into sections that you can work on one at a time. First, apply a contrasting coat of glaze over the base coat **(step 1)**. Do not worry about consistent brush strokes, as the ragging will work the glaze. Next, press a bunched-up piece of cloth into the wet glaze **(step 2)**. Move the cloth around in different directions to avoid creating a discernible pattern. Change to a clean cloth frequently. Don't continue to use a cloth when it has become engorged with glaze. The idea is to lift off glaze, exposing some of the base-coat color.

1 With a flat foam brush, apply a contrasting colored glaze over a thoroughly dry base coat.

2 Use a bunched-up soft cloth to lift off some of the glaze. Keep turning the cloth to avoid creating an obvious pattern.

An old metal bucket has been transformed with a ragged-on green-tinted glaze and lacquered vintage paper appliqués. The textured look of the ragging hides any signs of wear.

Painting Stripes and Plaids

You will need: Acrylic or latex paint for the base coat • Acrylic paint for the stripes • Flat foam paintbrushes • Fine artist's paintbrush: medium round • Sponge: natural or cellulose • Masking tape • Craft knife • Chalk pencil • Ruler or straightedge

Apply two base coats, and allow them to dry. The success of this technique depends largely on what you do before you begin to paint it. Measure the surface of the project, and then divide it into evenly distributed stripes. Mark their placement with a chalk pencil; then run a strip of masking tape along the outside edge of each one. To make the job easier, use masking tape that is the same width as the stripes, if possible. Smooth the tape down and burnish the edges with your fingers to secure it in place. Use a small piece of sponge or a foam brush to pull the paint over the unmasked area **(step 1)**. When the paint is thoroughly dry, remove the tape. Voilà, stripes! Creating a plaid design entails an additional step. Working perpendicular to the stripes you have just painted, mark new ones that can be the same or a different width as the originals. After masking the outside edges, paint the new stripes, which will intersect the first ones to form a crossbarred design **(step 2)**. Use the same color paint or a contrasting one. When the new paint dries thoroughly, remove the tape **(step 3)**.

1 After carefully measuring and masking, use a sponge or a foam brush to paint stripes.

2 Paint new stripes across the first ones to create a crossbarred pattern. Use the same color and stripe width for a checked plaid or various colors and widths for a traditional tartan look.

3 After the paint is completely dry, remove the tape. You can touch up any uneven edges with a fine artist's brush, or leave them as is.

Verdigris

You will need: Acrylic paints, including turquoise for the base; dark green, antique bronze, or copper for sponging • Flat foam paintbrushes • Fine artist's paintbrushes: medium round • One piece of natural sponge for each color paint • Paper towels

Paint the surface or object with two coats of the turquoise paint (the color of naturally occurring patina), and allow it to dry. Pour the other colors onto your palette. Lightly press the natural sponge into the green paint, and then dab the paint onto the surface **(step 1)**. Leave small areas of the turquoise base coat exposed. For an ideal effect, do not paint too much at this point; remember, you have to add more colors later. Change the direction of your sponge often to avoid a uniform pattern. Thin some dark green paint with water to create a wash. Using an artist's paintbrush, paint veins over the surface of the project **(step 2)**. Shake your hand, and twirl the paintbrush handle while painting to add a more natural flow. Finally, mottle the appearance by sponging on antique bronze or copper paint **(step 3)**. For realism, leave some areas alone.

1 Dab paint lightly over the object's surface, leaving some of the turquoise base coat exposed.

2 Draw veins over the surface using an artist's brush that has been dipped into a wash made with dark-green paint and water.

3 Mottle the look with random dabs of copper or bronze paint.

Hand Painting

You do not have to be an expert painter to experiment with some of the simple hand-painted motifs in this book. A delicate hand-painted border adds a special, one-of-a-kind quality to a finish and gives your work a professional appearance when it is combined with a decorative paint technique. It's worth spending some time experimenting with different artist's brushes on paper or on a wooden board until you become comfortable enough to add some unique detailing to one of your projects.

Simple Hand Painting

You will need: Acrylic paint in various colors • Fine artist's brushes, including flat, liner, pointed, and round in assorted sizes • Pencil • Sponge • Paper towels • Transfer paper

The most important advice about hand painting is to use high-quality artist's brushes. Cheap ones lose bristles and leave brush marks. Always practice on a board or paper before painting on the real surface **(step 1)**. Begin by marking the placement for the design and drawing it lightly with a pencil. Or you can use transfer paper to trace patterns from this book that you can carry to your project. Position the traced motif in place on your project, and slip a piece of transfer paper between the motif and the project. Retrace the lines of the motif, using a ballpoint pen to transfer it onto your project. Using an artist's flat or round paintbrush and the colors of your choice, dip the brush into the paint, and then dab off a bit. Gently guide the brush, allowing it to do the work, pressing down and easing up to vary the thickness of the line **(step 2)**. Keep a damp sponge and paper towels handy. If you make a mistake, wipe off the paint and try again.

1 It's an excellent idea to practice before attempting to hand paint a design on the actual surface you are decorating.

2 After lightly drawing or transferring a traced design onto your surface, allow the brush to do the work.

3 Finishes and Techniques

Stenciling

Stenciling is an excellent method for creating a repetitive pattern on a surface. Historically, it was the way middle-class people imitated the look of wallpaper, which once could be afforded only by the privileged.

With "positive stenciling," a template of the motif is cut into acetate or stencil paper. Paint is applied inside the cutout areas to transfer the image to a surface. With "negative stenciling," instead of painting inside a cutout shape, you paint around it. Remove the template, and the outline of the image remains on the surface.

Hand Painting from a Stencil

You will need: Assorted acrylic paint colors • Stencil brushes • Stencils • Ball-point pen • Spray adhesive • Fine artist's brushes: 1-inch flat, medium liner, medium round, #2 or #3 pointed • Paper towels • Chalk pencils • Ruler or straightedge

Paint the object or surface in any desired finish coat, and allow it to dry. Position the stencil on the surface to be decorated using spray adhesive to hold it in place. For extra support, tape it down. Using a pencil, trace the outlines of the stencil's shapes **(step 1)**. Once you've traced the entire design, remove the stencil template. Even though you will not paint the design entirely freehand, it's a good idea to practice on a board before attempting the real thing. This way, you can make brush strokes and create shading with confidence later.

Using artist's flat and round paintbrushes and the colors of your choice, fill in the outlined areas of the motif **(step 2)**. Double- or triple-load a flat paintbrush with different shades of color to add dimension. Use a stencil brush and a small amount of paint to create texture or a blush of color.

1 After mounting the stencil, trace the outlines of the design onto the object or surface you wish to paint.

2 Use an artist's brush to create shading on your design. This will give your work a professional appearance.

Positive Stenciling

You will need: Acrylic paints in assorted colors • Stencil blanks or paper • Stencil brushes • Tracing paper • Spray adhesive • Flat foam paintbrushes • Masking or painter's tape • Craft knife • Paper towels • Pencil • Ruler or straightedge

Paint the surface with two coats of the base color, and allow it to dry. Spray the reverse side of the stencil with spray adhesive to keep it from slipping while working. Position the template where you want the image to appear, and tape it in place. Dip the stencil brush into the paint, and then blot it on a paper towel **(step 1)**. The only trick involved with stenciling is to use a small amount of paint.

Stencil with one color of paint at a time. Mask any areas you are not working on. Pounce the brush up and down to make crisp, clean edges **(step 2)**. Work from the edges toward the center. You may blend the colors as you desire. Use lighter colors toward the center of the design, and make them darker toward the outside of the shape. You can create a hard edge or fade the paint into the background color. Use less paint, and build up layers for a clean professional-quality finish.

Always use a clean brush or a separate one for each color of paint you apply to your design **(step 3)**. Wipe off any excess paint from the template to prevent undesirable smears and smudges on your surface. Vary the direction of your motifs by reversing your stencil or positioning it at different angles. Let each layer of paint dry before applying another one.

1 Blot excess paint onto a paper towel to keep lines crisp. The key to expert stenciling is to use a tiny amount of paint.

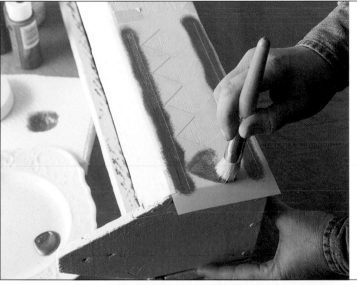

2 With the template securely in place, pounce on the paint using quick, stacatto movements.

3 Work from the edges to inside the cutout area, and always use a clean brush to apply each new color.

3 Finishes and Techniques

Negative Stenciling

You will need: Acrylic paint for a base coat • Contrasting color of spray paint • Desired distinctive flat shapes (such as leaf or fern) • Spray adhesive • Flat foam paintbrushes

Paint the surface with two coats of the base color, and allow it to dry. The base coat will be the color of the stenciled image. Spray the reverse side of your shapes with spray adhesive. Arrange them around the surface of your project **(step 1)**. Extend the shapes beyond your work surface to give partial shapes. Do not overlap the shapes, or they will lose their distinctive outlines. Press the shapes in place to keep spray paint from seeping underneath. Work in a well-ventilated space. Cover your work surface to protect it.

Following manufacturer's instructions and holding the spray-paint can 2 to 4 feet from the project, spray a fine mist of color onto the surface to cover it completely. Move the spray can back and forth to create an even and thorough coat. Spraying large amounts of paint will result in drips, so it is best to build up several layers, one at a time. When the paint is dry, remove the shapes **(step 2)**.

1 Arrange all of the shapes in a pleasing pattern; let some of them partially extend beyond the edges of the surface for a natural look.

2 The final effect. Don't use too much adhesive, or the forms will be difficult to remove after the spray paint has dried.

Great Stenciling

Don't be afraid to expand your ideas to painting a field of patterns on your walls and other surfaces. Wherever you can put paint, you can stencil a design. Stenciled motifs run from simple to complex, as do the color schemes with which you can apply them. Stencils are usually executed with one or two colors, but there are some complex patterns created with more than a dozen hues. However, such intricate designs may be overwhelming because they take a lot of time to apply and their complexity makes them confusing to paint because they require a separate stencil for each color. Designs with this degree of sophistication read better on large surfaces. If your home can carry off grandiose patterns, go for it—once you have become proficient and have the patience to work intricate motifs over the course of weeks or months. However, successful stenciling lies in the pattern, which is often simple and stylized. For the best results, stick with a motif that complements the style of your home and colors that coordinate with it.

Faux Stone

In the past, mimicking the look of stone surfaces with paint was a lengthy and often difficult process. Today, water-based paints and glazes have made applying a faux stone technique much easier for the average do it yourselfer.

When you are painting a faux stone, it helps to work from a sample of the real thing. Most stone tile stores will sell you a small piece. Use this as a guide for colors, shading, and patterning, such as marble veining. Experiment on a board before actually working on the real surface.

Malachite

You will need: Pale green acrylic craft paint • Dark green acrylic glaze • Rubber malachite paint comb • Flat foam paintbrushes • Paper towels

Paint the surface with two or more coats of the pale green paint base coat, and allow it to dry. Work one section at a time, as the technique requires that the top coat remain wet in order to manipulate it. With that in mind, apply a coat of the dark green glaze to one section of the surface. **(step 1)**. Wad up a paper towel, and gently pat the wet surface to remove some of the dark green glaze and to smooth out brush strokes **(step 2)**. Holding the combing tool at an 80-degree angle above the work surface, immediately drag it through the wet glaze. Make wavy, rounded motions, and apply pressure firmly as you cut through the glaze **(step 3)**. Keep your hand strokes smooth and steady as you create a shape that almost looks like the petals of a flower. Overlap the strokes as desired. If you make a mistake while the paint is still wet, just repaint and try again. Wipe the comb clean after each stroke to remove excess paint.

1 After the light-green base coat dries, apply a dark green glaze with a foam brush.

2 With a scrunched up paper towel, lift off some of the wet glaze and smooth over any brush strokes.

3 To create the malachite pattern, hold the comb at an 80-deg. angle and drag it firmly and evenly through the wet glaze, making half-round "petals."

Marbling

You will need: Four or more shades of acrylic paint, including black and white • Paint extender • Paint thickener • Denatured alcohol • Stippling brush • Spatter brush • Pointed goose feather • Flat foam paintbrushes • Fine artist's paintbrushes: medium round • Natural sponges • Paper towels • Ruler or straightedge

Use a real marble sample as a guide and for inspiration on color and veining patterns. Paint the project with two coats of the base color, and allow it to dry. Swirl circular loops of each of the paint colors and the white and black in your palette **(step 1)**. Swirl lines of thickener and extender over all of the paint. The extender will thin the colors, making them translucent. If the extender makes the paint runny, add thickener to the mixture so that you can work the technique. Gingerly dab the natural sponge into the paint; then lightly apply the color over the surface of the project **(step 2)**. Leave small areas where the base color shows through, resembling the grooves and crevices of natural marble. Combine colors, and overpaint or underpaint areas to mimic depth. Build up the layers, but never completely obscure the base coat in some areas. Change the direction of the sponge often to avoid a repetitious pattern.

1 With a marble tile sample nearby as your guide, swirl loops of paint colors on your palette.

2 Using a natural sponge, lightly dab paint onto the surface. Do not completely cover the base coat.

Keep your sponges clean of excess paint by washing them often. While the paint is still wet, dip the spatter brush in denatured alcohol, and tap the handle lightly with a ruler to spatter the surface **(step 3)**. Next, spatter the surface lightly with water, and allow it to sit for a few minutes; then wipe the water lightly with a sponge. This produces liquidlike shapes, creating an interesting and realistic pattern.

With a stippling brush, go over the surface to soften and blend some areas. Work the brush in a variety of directions **(step 4)**. Dip the point of the goose feather in the paints; then use it to paint veins over the surface of the project **(step 5)**. Barely touching the surface and shaking your hand, twirl the feather while painting to add a more natural appearance. However, these lines should tremble just slightly; don't make zigzags or squiggles. Paint veins in different colors and in different directions. Remember that veins don't crisscross like an X, and they don't end in sharp points like a triangle. They don't come to a sudden end, either. Rather, they move out to and off the edge of the surface. Highlight the veins with a fine paintbrush and contrasting or complementary colors. It's important to capture the variety in the veining patterns if you are painting a specific type of marble. It might be more helpful if you paint veins with various-sized small brushes. By constantly changing brushes, you will automatically vary the look of the veins you are painting. Finally, soften veins with the stippling brush.

3 Spatter denatured alcohol and water over the paint to make it form unusual, liquidlike patterns.

4 Use the stippling brush in random areas to soften the effect.

5 Using a feather, twirl color onto the surface to create veins.

3 Finishes and Techniques

Gilding

Traditional gilding requires an adhesive, called gold size, which takes many hours to become tacky enough for the metal leaf to adhere. It then begins to dry immediately, requiring the gilder to work quickly and nimbly. While this method is still used by most professionals, today there is a faster-drying, water-based variety of adhesive (or size) that is preferred by most do-it-yourselfers, who generally lack the time to wait all day to complete a project. The water-based size remains tacky long enough to work the technique, however, so there's no need to worry about speed of execution. Foils are also available; they come in silver, copper, and bronze. Each one produces an elegant look. When first applied, the metal leaf appears garish, but once it's rubbed with wax or shoe polish, it takes on a mellow sheen. Gilded items should be sealed with varnish or shellac so that they won't tarnish.

Use the rubbed gold finish to accent many of the projects. Simply rubbing a bit of golden wax along the edge of something adds a touch of class.

Gold Leafing

You will need: Acrylic paint for the base coat • Sheets of imitation gold leaf • Gold size (fast-drying variety) • Antiquing wax or brown shoe polish • Flat foam paintbrushes • Soft natural-bristle paintbrush • Small sheet of thin acetate or gilding tip • Talcum powder • Steel wool • Soft lint-free cloths • Shellac or spray varnish

1 Apply one or two base coats to the object or surface using a flat foam brush. Choose a color that will contrast well with the gold leaf, such as red oxide.

2 Apply the adhesive for the gold leaf with a soft, natural-bristle paint-brush; then let it dry to a tacky finish.

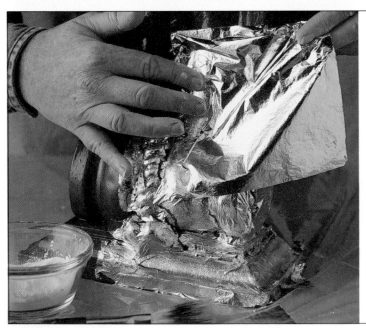

3 Use your hands to press the sheets of gold leaf onto the object or surface. Work it into crevices with the soft brush.

Work in a dust-free area away from open doors or windows. The sheets of gold leaf are delicate and will fly away in even a slight breeze. Using a foam paintbrush, paint the object with two or more coats of the base color, and allow it to dry **(step 1)**. The base coat will show through the fissures you will create in the gold leaf during the antiquing process later, so choose a color that will contrast well with gold, such as red oxide, terra cotta, dark green, or black. Smooth the surface of your project of any imperfections, such as paint drips, brush streaks, or hairs, with fine sandpaper or steel wool. The gold leaf is thin and will emphasize these imperfections rather than hide them. Gold leaf can be used as an all-over finish on any smooth surface or can be used sparingly as a decorative detail. If the surface or object you are decorating is large, work one small section at a time. Then, using the natural-bristle paintbrush, apply the transparent size **(step 2)**. When the surface feels tacky, cover it by hand with a sheet of the gold leaf **(step 3)**.

If you need more than one sheet, you can overlap them. (Dip your fingers in talcum powder so that the gold leaf does not stick to them.) Press the gold leaf into all of the crevices with the natural-bristle brush. You can smooth out the wrinkles and remove any excess by going over the surface of your project with a soft, lint-free cloth. Small cracks in the finish are desirable, however, and will allow the base coat to show through. Finally, rub antiquing wax or brown shoe polish over the entire surface with steel wool to tone it down and enrich the aging effect **(step 4)**.

4 With a piece of steel wool, rub antiquing wax or brown shoe polish all over the gold leafed surface.

Rubbing a Gold Finish

You will need: Gold wax • Soft, lint-free cloth

Rubbing on gold wax is a finishing technique, so before applying it, make sure the surface you will be working on is clean, dry, and already painted. You can use gold wax to highlight certain areas on a decorated surface. Rub wax onto selected areas of the finished surface using a soft, lint-free cloth or your finger. Work with the grain (if the surface is wood) or with the shape of the form or object.

Use your finger or a soft cloth to apply gold wax to selected areas you wish to highlight.

3 Finishes and Techniques

Stamped and Sponged Finishes

All of the stamping and sponging techniques are easy and fun to do. Rubber stamping and foam-shape stamping can be applied to a surface in a random or planned pattern.

Stamping can be used to create the effect of wallpaper. Depending on the design of the stamp itself, the results can look traditional, whimsical, or abstract. A fleur-de-lis motif that is applied in a regularly spaced pattern in gold on a navy blue background has a feeling totally different from that of multi-colored teacups floating haphazardly on a sky-blue background, for example. Likewise, the effect of overall sponging can vary greatly, depending on the colors you use and the density with which you apply the paint to the surface.

Stamping with Foam Shapes

You will need: Acrylic paint for the base coat • Acrylic glazes in assorted colors • Precut foam shapes • Flat paintbrushes • Fine artist's paintbrushes (½-inch flat) • Paper towels • Pencil

Paint the surface with two coats of the base color, and allow it to dry. Using the ½-inch flat artist's brushes, load the foam shapes with colored glazes **(step 1)**. Test the stamp on a sample board, first. Use more than one color on each stamp to add dimension. Press the stamp firmly onto the surface **(step 2)**. Overlap and change direction of the markings with each pass of the stamp, and vary the colors, if desired. By changing the angle of the stamps, you will create an almost three-dimensional look, which will add to the realism of the finished effect. You can also apply more pressure to one side of the stamp to create shading. Reload the stamp with paint for each application. If the image is too light, don't stamp over it. Instead, wipe off the wet paint with a moist paper towel, and then restamp when the area is dry. Keep in mind that a spontaneous approach works best. Don't worry about making each impression perfect. Variations make the look more interesting and natural. Wipe off or wash the stamp before applying a different paint color, and wait until each color dries before overlapping them—unless you want the colors to blend together.

1 Load the stamp with a colored glaze using a flat brush. You can apply one color or two.

2 Apply the wet stamp to the surface. Don't try to make each imprint uniform. It's okay to vary the density of paint and color.

Rubber Stamping

You will need: Acrylic paint for the base coat • Rubber stamps • Raised ink pad • Flat paintbrushes • Paper towels • Pencil • Ruler

Paint the surface or object with two coats of the base color, and allow it to dry. For an evenly spaced-out pattern, you'll have to measure the area, then decide how many passes with the stamp you'll need and how far apart to make each one. For a uniform design, note the position of each stamped image with a pencil. For a perfectly straight line, you could work with a straight edge as a guide if the surface you are covering is small. Otherwise, snap a chalk line to keep the design level. If you want to create a random pattern, rotate the stamp with each pass to change the direction of the motif. As with working with a foam stamp, you can add dimension and shading, if you like, by applying more or less pressure or by varying the amount of paint on the stamp. However, never overload the stamp or you will end up with just a blob of smeared paint. When you're ready to begin, load the rubber stamp with ink from the pad **(step 1)**. After making a test pass, press the stamp firmly onto the surface **(step 2)**. Reload with ink before each application of the stamp. Wash and dry the stamp before switching to a new color. When applying ink to the stamp, be sure to cover the raised design evenly each time so that you're not left with gaps in the impression.

1 Load the rubber stamp evenly with ink from an ink pad.

2 Holding the stamp, make a firm impression with it on the surface. Reload it with ink each time you make a new impression.

Sponging

You will need: Acrylic paint for the base coat, plus three or more additional colors for sponging • Flat foam brushes • Natural sponges • Paper towels • Painter's tape

Paint the object with two coats of the base color, and allow it to dry. Prepare a separate paint palette and sponge for each color. (With small objects, you can reuse a sponge by washing out the paint and wringing out excess moisture.) Experiment with different color combinations. Contrasting hues will produce a stronger look while related tones will have a subtler effect. Mask off areas where you do not want to apply paint. To begin, lightly dip the natural sponge into the first color; then dab it gingerly around the surface of the project **(step 1)**. Change the direction of the sponge often to avoid a repetitious pattern. Apply additional colors, one at a time **(step 2)**. For a more open and airy effect, do not apply dense layers of paint, but do feel free to overlap and blend colors. To sponge into corners, especially on a wall, cut off a small piece of the sponge to make a flat edge.

Create a softer variation by sponging off. That is a technique whereby you take a clean sponge and pounce it over a surface, randomly, removing some of the paint while it is still wet. Keep turning the sponge as you go. Once the sponge becomes engorged with paint, exchange it for a clean, dry one.

1 Load the sponge with a light coat of paint, and then gently dab it onto the surface.

2 Apply consecutive colors into areas that reveal only the base-coat color, but do not obscure it completely. To vary texture, use different-size sponges for each color.

Sponging Blocks

You will need: Acrylic paint for the base coat, plus assorted additional colors • Flat foam paintbrushes • Fine artist's paintbrushes: flat, liner, pointed, and round in assorted sizes • Cellulose kitchen sponges in desired size • Paper towels • Coated paper plates • Pencil • Ruler or straightedge

Paint the surface with two coats of the base color, and allow it to dry. The painted blocks will be the size of your sponge. If you want to create custom-size blocks for your surface, you can cut the sponges down. You may have to cheat a little if you cannot divide the surface into an even number of blocks. To make this less noticeable, begin your row in the center of the piece, and work toward the outside edges where a smaller end block is less noticeable than if it were to fall dead center. You can create straight rows of blocks or reproduce the stagger of a brick pattern.

Use a separate paper-plate palette and sponge for each color of paint. Wet each sponge with water and wring out the excess moisture. Press the sponge into the paint, and then offload some of the paint onto paper towels to avoid paint drips and runs. Firmly press the sponge onto the surface to make a clear impression **(step 1)**. Do the same thing with each alternating color, leaving about ¼ inch of space between each imprint **(step 2)**. Wipe drips with a damp sponge while the paint is still wet. Reload each sponge with paint and blot it before every application.

The blocks do not have to be perfect. Unevenness in the application of the paint and slightly wobbly edges will simply add charm and texture to the overall effect. Unlike a faux finish that should be as realistic as possible, creating blocks or bricks with a sponge is a technique that is intended to look hand painted.

1 Press a sponge that has been loaded with paint, and blotted, firmly onto the surface.

2 The final effect demonstrates consecutive rows of blocks in alternating colors. Leave a ¼-inch space between each block.

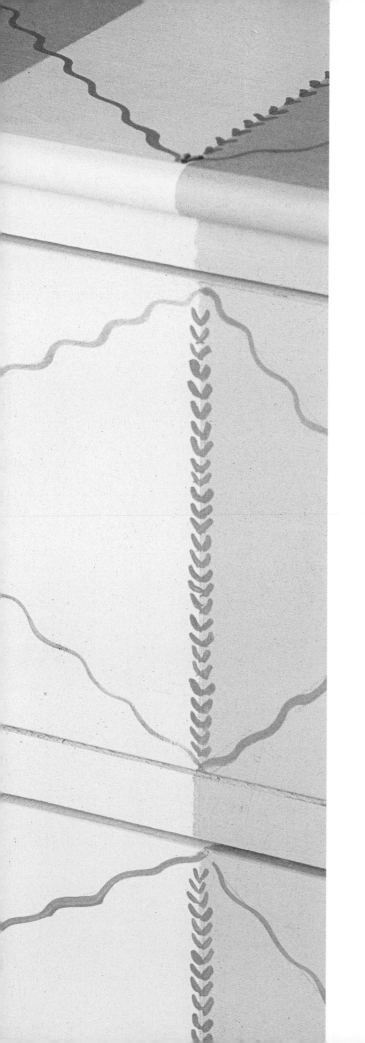

— part 2 —

paint projects

living room

Projects covered in this room setting: end table (page 51), fireplace screen (page 52), mantel planter (page 54), table lamp (page 55).

end table

Techniques

Distressing
page 29

Rubbing a Gold Finish
page 43

Marbling
page 40

Materials

- Unfinished wood table
- Primer
- Satin finish latex paint in off-white
- Acrylic craft paints in French Vanilla, Wicker White, Dapple Gray, and Caramel
- Decorator glazes in Tuscan Russet and Russet Brown
- Paint extender
- Paint thickener
- Metallic wax finish in

- Gold Classic
- Denatured alcohol
- Stippling brush
- Spatter brush
- Goose point feather
- Candle wax
- Antiquing wax or brown shoe polish
- Sandpaper and tack cloth
- Steel wool
- Multipurpose primer
- Flat foam paintbrushes

- Fine artist's paintbrushes, medium round
- Sponges, natural
- Masking tape
- Craft knife
- Mixing containers
- Paper towels
- Paper
- Soft lint-free cloths
- Pencil and scissors
- Ruler or straightedge
- Glossy sealer

Directions

1 Sand the table; wipe clean with a tack cloth; then apply one coat of primer. Let it dry. Rub the edges of the table legs and drawer knobs with candle wax, which will help simulate the uneven texture of age (Distressing, page 29).

2 Cover the table base with one coat of off-white paint. Allow it to dry, and then sand over the waxed areas to remove most of the paint. Rub antiquing wax or shoe polish over the surface. Following the directions for Rubbing a Gold Finish (page 43), massage gold wax over the knobs and edges of the table.

3 Paint the tabletop with two or more coats of French Vanilla paint. Let it dry. Following the directions for Marbling (page 40), paint a faux-marble finish on the tabletop. Apply two coats of a high-gloss sealer to make the tabletop look like polished stone.

fireplace screen

Techniques

Rubber Stamping
page 45

Positive Stenciling
page 37

Materials

- Wooden fireplace screen
- Primer
- Decorative base molding
- Satin finish latex paint in off-white
- Metallic acrylic craft paint in Gold and Antique Gold
- Decorator glazes in neutral, Italian Sage, Russet Brown, Sage Green, Ivy Green , Deep Woods Green, and Patina
- Stencils

- Ivy stamp
- Scroll stamp
- Antiquing medium in Apple Butter Brown
- Liquid leaf in Classic Gold
- 3-inch flat-bristle paintbrush
- Stencil brushes
- Waxed stencil paper
- Kraft paper
- Sandpaper and tack cloth
- Primer
- Flat foam paintbrushes

- Fine artist's paintbrushes: flat, liner, pointed, and round in assorted sizes
- Masking tape
- Craft knife, scissors
- Mixing containers
- Paper towels
- Pencil
- Straightedge
- Sealer

Directions

You'll need a hinged three-panel wooden fireplace screen, which you can buy or make. If you buy one, you'll have to sand and prime it thoroughly before applying the new finish over the existing one. Ideally, it's best to work on unfinished wood. The screen used for this project features two 9- x 36-inch side panels and one 26- x 36-inch center panel that were cut from a ¾-inch-thick sheet of plywood. If you aren't handy with a circular saw or table saw, ask your local lumber mill to cut the panels to your desired dimensions. Attach the side and center panels with two-way (piano) hinges, which are easy to install. Simply mark their location along the inside edges of the panel pieces, drill pilot holes, and then screw them into place.

1 Remove the hinges, and set them aside. Lightly sand the panels, and then wipe them clean with a tack cloth. Cut strips of 2-inch decorative base molding to fit the width of the panels, and glue the pieces along the bottom of each section. After the glue sets, apply two coats of primer to the panels. Let the primer dry, and then paint the panels with two coats of off-white latex paint.

2 Cut stencils for the topiary, roping, and lattice (pages 60-61), following directions for Making Your Own Stencil (page 36).

3 Draw a 3½-inch wide border along the top and both sides of the center panel, and along the tops and outer sides of the other two panels. Just below this border, draw a ½-inch-wide band at the top of the center panel and along the sides, top, and bottom of the other panels.

4 Arrange and mark the position of the topiary, roping, and lattice stencils on the panels. (You'll have to repeat the lattice down the length of each side panel.) Remove the stencil templates until later.

5 Mask the 3½-inch border and ½-inch band; then paint the middle section of each panel with the Apple Butter Brown antiquing medium. While the finish is still wet, rub some off with a soft cloth to make it look as though it has become slightly worn. After the medium dries, remove the tape.

6 Mix the Italian Sage and neutral glaze to your desired shade. Mask the inside and outside edges of the 3½-inch border. Apply the glaze inside the border on all panels, making crosshatched strokes with a 3-inch-wide flat brush. Let the glaze dry, and then remove the tape.

7 Mask the inside and outside edges of the ½-inch band; then fill it in with the Antique Gold using a ½-inch-wide flat brush. Let it dry, then remove the tape.

8 Measure and mark the placement of the border's stamped scroll motif. Following directions for Rubber Stamping (page 45), load the stamp with Antique Gold paint using a flat brush, and apply the design.

9 Following directions for Positive Stenciling (page 37), place the twisted-rope-pattern template into position on the panel, and apply the pattern using the Antique Gold paint. Remove the template. Stencil the lattice onto the side panels.

10 Stencil a large pot (page 61) in Gold, adding shading with an artist's brush and the Russet Brown. For the topiary, mix a tiny amount of green with the neutral glaze and paint one 5-inch and one 7½-inch round form (paint the smaller one above the other). Stencil the stem in Russet Brown. With the ivy stamp, fill in with leaves, overlapping and varying direction, using the three green glazes. Add veining with a fine artist's brush.

11 Highlight molding with the liquid leaf; apply two coats of sealer; and then reinstall the hinges.

Three-Dimensional Stenciling

A simple stenciled rope can be elevated to an artful three-dimensional rendering by shading with several values of one color. You'll need a separate cutout pattern for each shade. For this design, light, medium, and dark gray provide the palette.

mantel planter

Techniques

Positive Stenciling
page 37

Rubber Stamping
page 45

Rubbing a Gold Finish
page 43

Materials

- Wooden feedbox
- Primer
- Satin finish latex paint in off-white
- Metallic acrylic craft paint in Gold and Solid Bronze
- Stencil
- Metallic gold wax

- Rubber stamp
- Gold raised ink stamp pad
- Stencil brushes
- Spray adhesive
- Sandpaper and tack cloth
- Steel wool
- Heavy-duty primer
- Flat foam paintbrushes

- Masking or painter's tape
- Craft knife
- Paper towels
- Soft lint-free cloths
- Pencil
- Ruler or straightedge
- Sealer

Directions

1 Sand the box, and then wipe it clean with a tack cloth. Apply one or two coats of primer as needed. Let it dry. Paint the box with two coats of off-white paint.

2 When the box is dry, arrange a diamond-and-line border stencil on its front and side panels, and mark the placement. Referring to the photo, above right, for placement, stencil every other diamond and all of the line borders with Gold paint (Positive Stenciling, page 37).

3 Wait for the paint to dry before stenciling the remaining diamonds with Solid Bronze paint. Make note of a place in the center along the top edge of the front panel and on the sides of the planter for the star design. Apply the gold stars (Rubber Stamping, page 45). Following the directions for Rubbing a Gold Finish (page 43), rub gold wax along the edges of the box. Finish it with two coats of sealer.

table lamp

Techniques

Positive Stenciling
page 37

Rubber Stamping
page 45

Rubbing a Gold Finish
page 43

Materials

- Unfinished wooden lamp base
- Self-adhesive lampshade, 8 x 14 x 11 inches
- Fabric with topiary print
- 1¼ yards of fringe trim in a shade to match the fabric
- ¾ yard of flat braid trim in a shade to match the fabric
- Hot-glue gun and glue sticks
- Metallic acrylic craft paint in French Vanilla, Antique Gold, and Old Ivy
- Decorator glaze in Russet Brown, Italian Sage, Deep Woods Green, and Patina
- Lattice stencil
- Antiquing medium in Brown
- Liquid leaf in Classic Gold
- Stencil blanks or paper
- Stencil brushes, rubber eraser
- Transfer paper
- Spray adhesive
- Sandpaper and tack cloth
- Steel wool
- Multipurpose primer
- Flat foam paintbrushes
- Masking tape, craft knife
- Paper towels, lint-free cloths
- Pencil, ruler, scissors

Directions

1 Sand the lamp base to create a smooth surface. Wipe it with a tack cloth, and then apply two coats of the primer. Paint the two sides, flat bottom, and top of the base with two coats of Old Ivy paint. Let the paint dry.

2 Mask the edges of the green areas, and then paint the front and back panels with two coats of French Vanilla paint. Let it dry.

3 Apply antiquing medium to the front and back panels. While the medium is still wet, rub some off with a soft cloth. Remove the tape.

4 On a photocopier, resize the topiary and lattice stencils to a size suitable for your lamp base. Following the directions for Positive Stenciling (page 37), create the topiary for the front panel, beginning with the container, which is applied with the Antique Gold paint, then the stem, using the Russet Brown glaze.

5 For the round topiary forms, use a pale mixture of the green and neutral glazes applied with an artist's brush. Paint one above the other, making the top form smaller than the other, as shown in the photo.

6 With a craft knife, cut a small leaf shape into an ordinary rubber pencil eraser. Following the directions for Rubber Stamping (page 45), load and off-load the carved eraser with the various green glazes and randomly fill in the topiary balls with leaves. Repeat the design on the back panel.

7 Stencil the lattice on each of the green-painted side panels in Antique Gold.

8 Following the directions for Rubbing a Gold Finish (page 43), rub gold wax along the edges of the lamp's base. In this case, the base is attached to four wooden balls, which have been painted with liquid gold leaf. Finish the lamp base with two or more coats of sealer.

Projects covered in this room setting: malachite box (page 57), golden bookends (page 58), desk lamp (page 59).

malachite box

Techniques

Malachite
page 39

Rubbing a Gold Finish
page 43

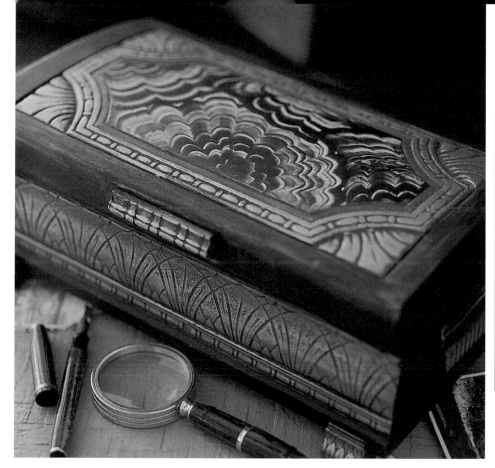

Materials

- Carved wooden box
- Primer
- Acrylic craft paint in Brick Red and Pale Green
- Dark Green acrylic glaze
- Rubber malachite paint comb

- Metallic wax finish in Renaissance Gold
- Sandpaper and tack cloth
- Steel wool
- Fine artist's paint brush, ½" flat
- Flat paintbrushes: foam or bristle

- Masking or painter's tape
- Craft knife
- Paper
- Soft lint-free cloths
- Ruler or straightedge
- Sealer

Directions

1 Sand the box to create a smooth surface, and then wipe it with a tack cloth. Apply one or more coats of the primer to the entire surface, covering the lid and all four sides.

2 When the primer dries, mask the four sides of the box. Cover the lid with at least two coats of Pale Green paint. Let it

dry. Then coat it with the Dark Green glaze, and following the directions for Malachite (page 39), work the technique over the area. Allow the Malachite to dry, and then mask it.

3 Unmask the four sides of the box; then coat them with Brick Red paint. Apply the Dark Green glaze to the edges of the lid.

Following the directions for Rubbing a Gold Finish (page 43), rub gold wax over the relief-patterned edges. Remove masking tape from the Malachite.

4 Finish the box with two or more coats of sealer.

golden bookends

Techniques

Gold Leafing
page 42

Materials

- Plaster bookends
- Acrylic craft paint in Brick Red
- Sheets of imitation gold leaf
- Gold leaf adhesive

- Antiquing wax or brown shoe polish
- Soft natural-bristle paintbrush
- Talcum powder

- Multipurpose or heavy-duty primer
- Flat paintbrushes: natural bristle
- Soft lint-free cloths

Directions

1 Wipe off the bookends to remove surface dust or grime, and then prepare them for refinishing with one or more coats of primer. If the surface is less than perfect, all the better for a vintage appearance.

Let the primer dry before applying two or more coats of Brick Red paint. Allow the paint to dry.

2 Following the directions for Gold Leafing (page 42), add

gilding to the bookends. (You don't need a uniform finish.)

3 Rub them with antiquing wax or shoe polish, and then apply two coats of sealer.

desk lamp

Techniques

Verdigris
page 34

Rubbing a Gold Finish
page 43

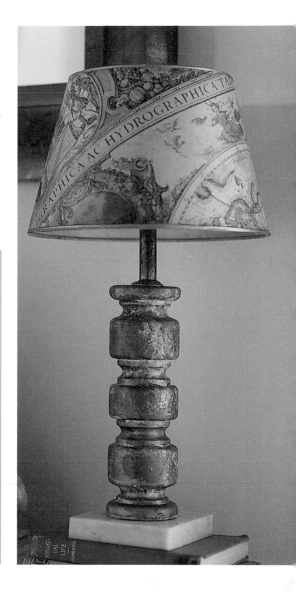

Materials

- Wooden lamp base
- Paper lampshade
- Acrylic craft paint in Patina and Old Ivy
- Metallic acrylic craft paint in Antique Copper and Solid Bronze
- Tissue wrapping paper in Old World map print
- Metallic wax finish in Classic Gold
- Spray adhesive
- Large sheet of paper
- Sandpaper and tack cloth
- Multipurpose or heavy-duty

- primer
- Flat paintbrushes, foam or bristle
- Fine artist's paintbrush, medium round
- Natural sponge
- Masking or painter's tape
- Craft knife
- Paper towels
- Kraft paper
- Soft lint-free cloths
- Pencil
- Ruler or straightedge
- Scissors
- Spray sealer

Directions

1 Sand the lamp base to create a smooth surface. Wipe it clean with a tack cloth. Cover any areas not to be painted with masking tape.

2 Apply one or more coats of primer. Let it dry. Following the directions for Verdigris (page 34), coat the base until you have achieved the desired patina effect. Allow the finish to dry.

3 Highlight some areas with gold wax (Rubbing a Gold Finish, page 43).

4 Make a pattern for the lampshade. Place the shade on a large sheet of kraft paper, and then roll it, tracing the top and bottom edges as you go around the diameter of each. The result is a flat curved pattern that you can cut out and use as a template. Fit it around the lampshade; secure it with a paper clip; and then make any necessary adjustments, such as trimming away excess paper.

5 Using the paper pattern, cut a piece of decorative tissue paper to the same dimensions. Spray the back side of the tissue paper with spray adhesive, and then place it onto the shade, smoothing as you go. If desired, glue fabric trim along the edges or rub in gold wax.

6 Finally, seal both the lampshade and the lamp base.

patterns

Follow the directions for Making
Your Own Stencil (page 36) using
these patterns as a guide. Enlarge or
reduce these images on a copier to
make them the correct scale for your
project.

Topiary Globes

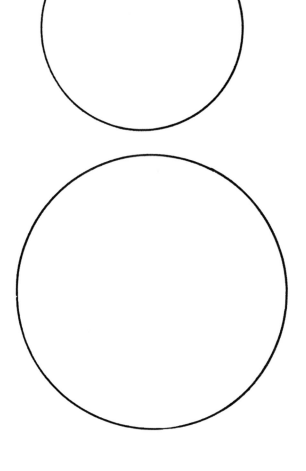

Diamonds

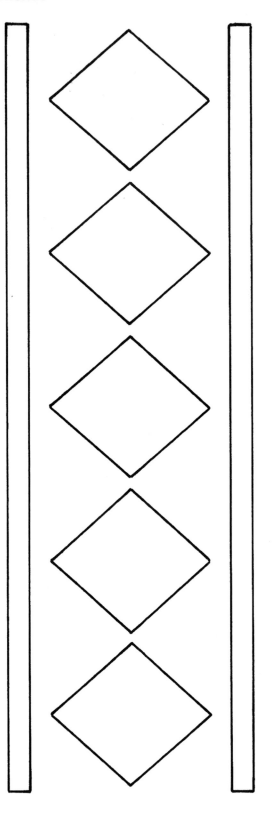

Roping

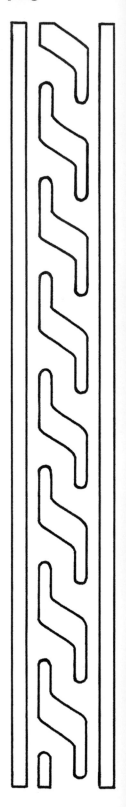

Large Pot

Lattice

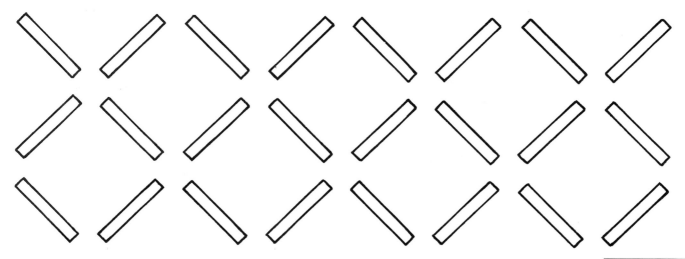

kitchen

Projects covered in this room setting: plaid-painted vegetable stools (page 63), stenciled bread box (page 64), sponged and stenciled silverware caddy (page 65).

plaid-painted vegetable stools

Techniques

Painting Stripes and Plaid
page 33

Materials

- 3 unfinished wooden kitchen stools
- Latex paint in Linen White
- Acrylic craft paint in Sterling Green, Poppy Red, and Mystic Green
- Decoupage medium

- Vegetable-print motifs cut out from wallpaper or decorative paper
- Flat foam paintbrushes
- Sandpaper and tack cloth
- Masking or painter's tape
- Craft knife

- Ruler or straightedge
- Sponge, natural or cellulose
- Pencil
- Cardboard tube from paper towel roll
- Sealer

Directions

1 Sand the stools to create a smooth surface. Prime the stools; then paint them with two coats of the Linen White paint. Let the paint dry.

2 Follow the directions for Painting Stripes and Plaid (page 33), using a different shade of the acrylic paint for each stool seat.

3 Coat the reverse sides of the cutouts with decoupage medium. Press them onto the seats, and go over them with another coat of the medium.

4 To create a scalloped border, pour a small amount of the Linen White paint onto a paper plate. Dip half of one end of a cardboard tube into the paint. Using the photo above as a guide and the tube as a stamp, transfer the paint to the stools, reloading when necessary and working the design all the way around each of the seat tops. When the paint is dry, finish the stools with two or more coats of non-yellowing sealer.

stenciled bread box

Techniques

Dragging
page 30

Hand Painting from a Stencil
page 36

Sponging Blocks
page 47

Materials

- Unfinished wooden hinged-lid bread box
- All-purpose primer
- Acrylic craft paint in Purple, Crimson, Poetry Green, Lemon Custard, Harvest Gold, Sunny

- Yellow, and Burnt Sienna
- Decorator glaze in Sunflower
- Fruit border stencil
- Small foam sponge
- Artist's brushes: #3 round and ½-inch flat

- Dragging brush
- Flat foam paintbrushes
- Pencil
- Sandpaper and tack cloth
- Sealer

Directions

1 Sand the bread box to create a smooth surface, and wipe it with a tack cloth. Mask the hinges, and then prime the box. When the primer is dry, apply two coats of Lemon Custard paint. Let it dry.

2 Following the directions for Dragging (page 36), apply the technique using the Sunflower glaze. Let it dry.

3 Transfer the fruit motif to the lid of the bread box using the assorted acrylic paints and following the directions for Hand Painting from a Stencil (page 36). Refer to the photo, above right, as a guide for positioning.

4 To create the checkerboard pattern, follow the directions for Sponging Blocks (page 47), and

apply the pattern along the edge of the box with Burnt Sienna paint. Use a straightedge as a guide for the top row of blocks. (Make sure that the blocks in the top row are directly above the spaces in the first row.)

5 Finish the bread box with two or more coats of sealer.

sponged & stenciled silverware caddy

Techniques

Sponging Blocks
page 47

Positive Stenciling
page 37

Materials

- Unfinished wooden tool caddy
- Acrylic craft paint in Crimson, Buttercream, Poetry Green, Red Orange, and Harvest Gold
- Fruit stencils
- Foam sponges
- Flat foam paintbrushes
- Sandpaper and tack cloth
- Pencil
- Artist's liner brush
- Sealer

Directions

1 You don't have to have an old wooden tool caddy for your project. In fact, it's easier to work with a new, unfinished version, which you can purchase at a craft shop. Either way, make sure the wood is dirt-free, but go over the edges with sand-paper to create a slightly distressed vintage appearance.

2 Apply two coats of the Buttercream paint to both the outside and interior sections of the caddy. Let the paint dry.

3 Following the directions for Sponging Blocks (page 47), apply a small checkerboard pattern along the sides and handle using

the Harvest Gold paint. Following the directions for Positive Stenciling (page 37), create the fruit motif using the red and green paints. With an artist's brush, apply a thin green line freehand along the edges of the handle. Finish with two coats of sealer.

patterns

Follow the directions for Making Your Own Stencil (page 36) using these patterns as a guide. Enlarge or reduce these images on a copier to make them the correct scale for your project.

Flower

Pear

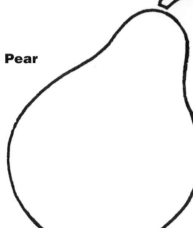

Grapes

Plums

Cherries

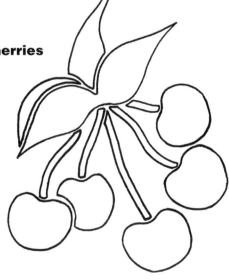

Apple

Fruit Border

chapter 6

bedroom

Projects covered in this room setting: floral headboard (page 69), striped dresser (page 70).

floral headboard

Techniques

Sponging
page 46

Simple Hand Painting
page 35

Rubbing a Gold Finish
page 43

Paper Cutouts

Materials

- Wooden headboard
- Latex satin paint in green
- Acrylic craft paint in Cappuccino, Poetry Green, Green Meadow, and Taffy
- Floral wallpaper
- Decoupage medium
- Metallic wax finish in Renaissance

- Sandpaper
- Steel wool
- Tack cloth
- Heavy-duty primer
- Flat paintbrushes: foam or bristle
- Fine artist's paintbrushes: #4 liner, medium pointed
- One natural sponge for each color

- paint
- Chalk pencil
- Painter's tape
- Craft knife
- Paper towels, lint-free cloths
- Pencil, ruler
- Sharp-pointed scissors
- Sealer

Directions

1 Sand the headboard, and then apply two coats of primer. Let it dry; then apply two coats of the satin green base.

2 Mask the frame. Following the directions for Sponging (page 46), sponge-paint the center panel with Taffy, Cappuccino, and Poetry Green paint. Let it dry.

3 Cut out three large and two small floral motifs from the wallpaper. Once the paint has

dried, you can arrange the paper cutouts inside the center panel. Mark their placement with the chalk pencil. Coat them on the reverse side with decoupage medium, then put them in place, carefully smoothing out any wrinkles or air bubbles. Go over them with one or two more coats of the decoupage medium. Let them dry.

4 Remove the masking tape from the frame of the headboard, then carefully mask the center panel.

5 Draw a wavy chalk line down the center. Following directions for Simple Hand Painting (page 35), use the Green Meadow acrylic paint and the pointed brush to create small leaves on either side of the wavy line. Use the liner brush over the chalk line and connect the leaves.

6 Following the directions for Rubbing a Gold Finish (page 43), embellish the edges of the frame and posts. Remove the tape. Finish with two coats of sealer.

6 Bedroom

striped dresser

Techniques

Simple Hand Painting
page 46

Materials

- Three-drawer unfinished wood dresser
- Latex satin paint in cream and green
- Acrylic craft paint in Portrait Light, Naphthol Green, Poetry Green, Mystic Green, Old Ivy, and Burgundy
- Sandpaper and tack cloth
- Steel wool
- Multipurpose primer
- Flat foam paintbrushes
- Fine artist's paintbrushes: flat, liner, pointed, and round in assorted sizes
- Masking or painter's tape
- Craft knife
- Paper towels
- Chalk pencil
- Ruler or straightedge
- Sealer

Directions

1 Remove all drawers and hardware from the dresser. Sand the dresser and drawers to create a smooth surface. Wipe them clean with a tack cloth, and then apply two coats of the primer.

2 To create the stripes, replace the drawers, and then divide the top and front of the dresser into an odd number of vertical panels. Mark them with a straightedge and a chalk pencil. In the same manner, mark out stripes along the sides of the dresser.

3 Remove the drawers to make painting easier. Beginning with the center stripe, run a line of masking tape along the outside edges of every other stripe. Smooth down and burnish the edges of the tape with your fingers to secure it in place.

4 Using a wide foam brush, paint the center and every alternate stripe with two or more coats of the green satin latex paint. Allow it to dry.

5 Remove the tape, and then mask the alternate stripes in the same manner.

6 Paint these stripes with a clean foam brush using two or more coats of the cream paint. Let it dry. Remove the masking tape.

7 To create the trellis design, divide the drawer panels into three sections. The center section should consist of three stripes, with two stripes comprising the sections to the left and right of the center.

8 Make a straight line along the outside edges of each center section. Within each section, draw a line from each corner to the opposite one; then make a small "+" in the middle of each section.

9 Thin the Poetry Green paint with a small amount of water. Following directions for Simple Hand Painting (page 46), create tiny leaves along the first lines using the pointed brush. Then paint wavy lines along each "X" with a liner brush. Arrange the leaves staggered or emanating in a straight line.

10 Using a round brush, make small Burgundy rosebuds or bouquets in the center of the "+." Use all the colors in your palette for the flowers and double- or triple-load your paintbrush to add dimension and shades. Add the leaves at all four points of the "+."

11 Divide the top and sides of the dresser in half lengthwise to paint the trellis . Make a large flower arrangement in the center of the dresser top.

12 When your hand painting dries, apply two or more coats of sealer to the entire piece.

Painting Stripes

Stripes are among the most attractive painted effects you can add to a surface. Broad, even stripes, such as the ones used on the dresser featured in this chapter, can go on fairly quickly and evenly. If your hand isn't particularly steady, you may want to roll on the paint rather than use a brush to apply it. You can find narrow rollers in paint and craft shops, or you can cut down a standard-size roller to the desired width of the stripe. It's best to use a thick paint because you have to make one uninterrupted pass with the roller. Avoid running the roller up and down.

Load the roller from a paint tray. Start at the top, and run the roller straight down (or across) the surface. For a neat look, mask the edges before applying the paint.

6 Bedroom

garden room

Projects covered in this room setting: fern floor cloth (page 73).

fern floor cloth

Techniques

Sponging
page 46

Negative Stenciling
page 38

Materials

- Unprimed heavyweight canvas
- Acrylic craft paint in Sunflower and Poetry Green
- Spray paint in Corn Silk
- Dried and pressed fern fronds
- Spray adhesive

- White glue
- Rolling pin
- Kraft paper or plastic wrap
- Flat foam paintbrushes
- Sponges, natural
- Masking or painter's tape

- Craft knife
- Paper towels
- Pencil
- Ruler or straightedge
- Scissors
- Sealer

Directions

1 Cut a rectangle of heavyweight canvas. Fold over 1½ inches of the cloth on all four sides. Miter the the corners, and glue "the hem" to the underside.

2 Cover a rolling pin with plastic wrap, and use it to smooth the hem in place. Finish with several coats of sealer.

3 Paint the canvas with two or more coats of Poetry Green paint. Let it dry.

4 Measure and mark a 1-inch border around all four sides. Run a line of masking tape along the edge next to the main section.

5 Following the directions for Sponging (page 46), lightly sponge enough yellow paint on the border. Let it dry, and then remove the masking tape and paper.

6 Measure and mark a second, wider border that's 8 inches from the inside edge of the one you just painted.

7 Draw an 8-inch square in each corner. Mask and cover both borders, except the corner squares.

8 Using spray adhesive, randomly mount the fern fronds in the corner squares and inside the main section of the cloth.

9 Following directions for Negative Stenciling (page 38), spray these areas with Corn Silk paint. Let the paint dry; then remove the masking tape and the fronds. Apply sealer.

chapter 8

child's room

Projects covered in this room setting: sponge-block toy chest (page 75), table and chairs (page 76), ark peg shelf (page 77).

sponge-block toy chest

Techniques

Sponging Blocks
page 47

Materials

- Unfinished pine blanket chest
- Latex paint in off-white
- Acrylic craft paint in Sterling Blue, Cappuccino, and Dapple Gray
- Acrylic gloss paint in Laguna Blue
- Upholstery foam, 3 inches thick
- Noah's Ark-motif fabric

- Decorative trim
- Fabric glue
- Sharp serrated knife
- Staple gun
- Sandpaper and tack cloth
- Multipurpose primer
- Flat foam paintbrushes
- One cellulose sponge for

each brick color
- Masking or painter's tape
- Craft knife
- Paper towels
- Chalk pencil
- Ruler or straightedge
- Scissors
- Sealer

Directions

1 Sand the trunk. Apply two coats of primer; let it dry; and then follow with two coats of off-white paint. Let it dry.

2 Measure each side. Divide the panels to establish a grid.

3 Mark the placement of the sponge blocks on the sides of the trunk with a chalk pencil and a straightedge, leaving about a ¼-inch space between each one. Because the blocks don't have to be perfectly aligned, use your eye to establish the spacing between each one.

4 Following the directions for Sponging Blocks (page 47), apply the various paint colors randomly. Start at the center; then continue to the right and left. If your calculations come up a bit short, you can cheat on the size of the blocks at the end of the row.

5 Let it dry. Apply two coats of sealer.

6 To make the cushion, take a piece of fabric that's large enough to cover upholstery foam cut to fit the top of the trunk.

7 Position the foam on the top of the trunk lid. Fold the fabric over the foam to the back side of the trunk top.

8 Work from the center out toward the sides, smoothing wrinkles, and staple it onto the lid.

9 Miter the fabric at the corners of the trunk top.

10 Glue trim along the edge of the trunk top.

table & chairs

Techniques

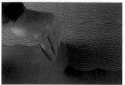

Combing
page 27

Positive Stenciling
page 37

Materials

- Unpainted wooden child's table and chairs
- Acrylic craft paint in Patina, Buttercup, Licorice, and Coffee Bean
- Decorator glaze in neutral and Plate Blue
- Noah's Ark stencil
- Noah's Ark-motif wallpaper

- Decoupage medium
- Rubber multipurpose paint comb
- Stencil brushes
- Spray adhesive
- Sandpaper and tack cloth
- Multipurpose primer
- Flat foam paintbrushes
- Sponges: natural

- Masking or painter's tape
- Craft knife
- Mixing container
- Paper towels
- Soft lint-free cloths
- Chalk pencil
- Ruler or straightedge
- Sharp-pointed scissors
- Sealer

Directions

1 Sand the table and chairs, and wipe them with a tack cloth. Apply one or more coats of primer, let it dry, then follow with two coats of Patina paint for the base. Let it dry.

2 Mix the neutral glaze with Plate Blue glaze until you get the desired shade. Use a sponge to apply an uneven coat to the table and chair. The green glaze that's applied to two of the chair's back spokes can be made by adding some of the Buttercup paint to the blue glaze mixture.

3 While the glaze is still wet and following the directions for Combing (page 27), use the paint comb to create the patterns. On the tabletop, work it in a wavy motion. On the chair seat, work it vertically, and then go over it again horizontally to make a checked pattern. On the flat back panel of the chair, comb alternating blocks of vertical and horizontal strokes. Let the glaze dry thoroughly.

4 Coat the reverse side of the ark and animal cutouts with decoupage medium and lightly press them in place, carefully smoothing out any wrinkles or air bubbles. Go over the facing sides with one or two coats of decoupage medium.

5 Following the directions for Positive Stenciling (page 37), add the words "Two by Two" with Licorice and Coffee Bean paints. Apply two coats of sealer to both pieces.

ark peg shelf

Techniques

Frottage
page 31

Positive Stenciling
page 37

Materials

- Unfinished wooden peg shelf, 24 inches wide
- Acrylic craft paint in Dark Gray, Terra Cotta, Cappuccino, Blue Ribbon, Evergreen, Wicker White, Buttercup, and Coffee Bean
- Noah's Ark stencil
- Stencil brushes

- Spray adhesive
- Newspaper or plastic wrap
- Sandpaper and tack cloth
- Multipurpose primer
- Flat foam paintbrushes
- Fine artist's paintbrushes
- Masking or painter's tape
- Craft knife

- Mixing containers
- Paper towels
- Pencil
- Ruler or straightedge
- Scissors
- Sealer

Directions

1 Remove the pegs from the shelf. Sand the shelf and the pegs. Apply primer; let it dry; and then follow with two coats of Cappuccino paint for the base. Let it dry.

2 Thin the blue paint with water. Following the directions for Frottage (page 31), coat the shelf with the thinned blue paint and work the technique. Rub the pegs with the thinned blue paint for an uneven finish.

3 Position the desired animal stencils across the shelf, and mark their placement; then follow the directions for Positive Stenciling (page 37). Use Coffee Bean paint for the ark, Buttercup paint for the roof and the giraffe's body, and Terra Cotta paint for the animal's spots. The alligators should be rendered in Evergreen and the elephants in Dark Gray. Stencil the clouds with Wicker White paint.

4 Let the paints dry, and then replace the pegs. Finish two coats of sealer.

patterns

Follow the directions for Making Your Own Stencil (page 36) using these patterns as a guide. Enlarge or reduce these images on a copier to make them the correct scale for your project.

Ark

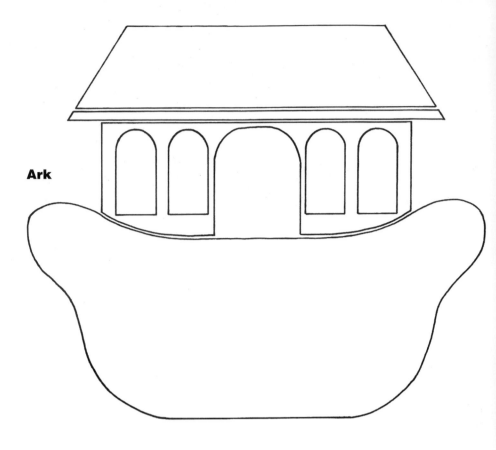

Camel

Bird

Rabbit

Zebra

Elephant

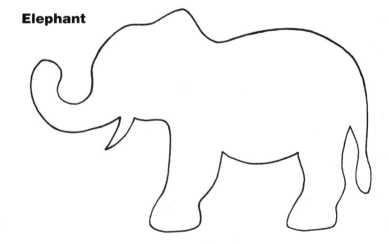

Acetate A plastic sheet material often used for making stencils.

Acrylic paint A water-soluble paint with a plastic polymer (acrylic) binder.

Aniline dyes Any of numerous synthetic dyes. Aniline dyes were developed in Germany in 1856.

Artist's oil paint Pigment suspended in linseed oil. It comes in a tube and in a wide range of saturated colors.

Blender brushes Specialty brushes used to blend and soften all types of wet painted surfaces.

Cheesecloth A loosely woven, coarse cotton gauze used to create different textures as well as to blend and smooth wet paint over a surface.

Cheesecloth distressing The technique of blending and softening wet paint strokes and colors by pouncing bunched-up cheesecloth over a surface.

Clear top coat A transparent finishing layer of protection applied over a decorated surface.

Color scheme A group of colors used to create visual harmony in a space.

Color washing The technique of applying layers of heavily thinned glaze to a surface.

Combing A technique that involves dragging a plastic or metal comb through wet paint or glaze in order to simulate texture or to create a pattern.

Contrast The art of assembling colors with different values and intensities and in different proportions to create a dynamic scheme.

Decoupage The technique of applying cut-out paper or fabric motifs to a surface, and then coating the images with varnish or decoupage medium.

Decoupage medium A smooth and glossy gluelike liquid used to apply cut-out paper or fabric images to a surface or an object. It is used as both an adhesive and a top coat.

Dragging A technique that involves pulling a special long-bristled brush through wet paint or glaze to create fine lines or narrow stripes.

Faux The French word for "false." With regard to painted finishes, it is used to describe any technique in which paint is manipulated on a surface to imitate the appearance of another substance, such as wood or stone.

Ferrule The metal part of a paintbrush that holds the bristles to the handle.

Flogger/dragger A wide, long-bristled brush that can be dragged through or slapped over wet paint or glaze to simulate texture or to create a pattern.

Glaze A thinned-down, translucent emulsion that may or may not contain pigment (color).

Graining comb A flexible steel or plastic device with random-sized tines or teeth. It is dragged through wet glaze or paint to create striated or grained surfaces. A common hair comb makes a workable substitute.

Latex paint A water-soluble, fast-drying paint that contains either acrylic or vinyl resins or a combination of the two. High-quality latex paints contain 100-percent acrylic resin.

Lining brush A thin, flexible, long-bristled brush used for finelining and detail work.

Negative stenciling Creating an image by blocking areas on a surface with a form or shape and then painting around it. The shape of the image remains on the surface after the form is removed.

Negative technique Any painting technique that involves removing wet paint or glaze from a surface. It is also called a "subtractive technique."

Overglaze A thin glaze added as a final step to a decorative finish. It can be a thinner version of either the base-coat color or another hue.

Palette Traditionally, a small wooden board for mixing dollops of paint. It can also be made of plastic or improvised using a glass, plastic, or plastic-coated-paper plate.

Palette knife An artist's knife with a thin, dull, flexible blade used for mixing, scraping, or applying paint. It can be made of plastic or metal.

Positive stenciling Creating an image or a motif, often in a repeated pattern, by painting inside a cut-out pattern.

Positive technique Any painting technique that involves applying paint to a surface.

Primers Primers prepare surfaces for painting by making them more uniform in texture and giving tooth.

Ragging off The technique in which paint is pulled from a surface with a bunched-up cloth. Sometimes called "cheeseclothing."

Ragging on The technique in which paint is applied to a surface with a bunched-up cloth.

Sea sponge A natural sponge, not to be confused with the cellulose variety.

Sealer A coating that is applied over a porous surface to form a durable, non-absorbent barrier between the surface and paint.

Shade A color to which black has been added to make it darker.

Sponging A paint technique that involves using a sponge to apply or take off paint.

Stencil A cut-out pattern.

Tint A color to which white has been added to make it lighter.

Tone A color to which gray has been added to change its value.

index